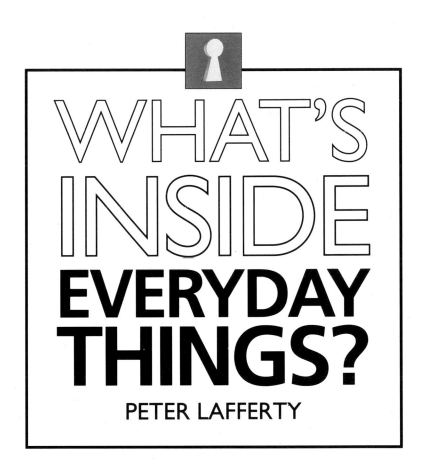

WHAT'S INSIDE EVERYDAY THINGS?

PETER LAFFERTY

PETER BEDRICK BOOKS
2112 Broadway
New York, NY 10023

Published by
PETER BEDRICK BOOKS
2112 Broadway
New York, NY 10023

© 1993 Macdonald Young Books Ltd.

Published by agreement with Macdonald
Young Books Ltd, England.

Library of Congress Cataloging-in-
Publication Data

Lafferty, Peter.
What's inside everyday things? / Peter Lafferty. —
1st Amer. ed.   p.   cm.—(What's inside series)
Includes index.
ISBN 0-87226-396-7
1. Machinery—Juvenile literature. [1. Machinery.]
I. Title. II. Series.
TJ147.L24   1995
821.8—dc20
95-2060
CIP
AC

Commissioning Editor: Thomas Keegan
Designer: John Kelly
Editor: Nicky Barber
Illustrators: Brian Watson, David Cook
(Linden Artists): Maltings Partnership;
Kevin Maddison
Typesetter:
Goodfellow & Egan, Cambridge

First American edition 1995
Printed and bound in Hong Kong

Words in bold in the text can be found in
the Glossary on p.44

Contents

The electric house

The modern Swiss architect, Le Corbusier, said that a house is a machine for living in. Like all machines, a house is made up of different parts, or systems, linked together. A house has a heating system, perhaps an air conditioning system, a water system, a waste disposal system and an electricity supply system. To live in comfort, we must have a safe supply of electricity.

Electric sockets are connected to the power supply by a cable which leaves the circuit breaker panel or fuse box and passes through each outlet in turn.

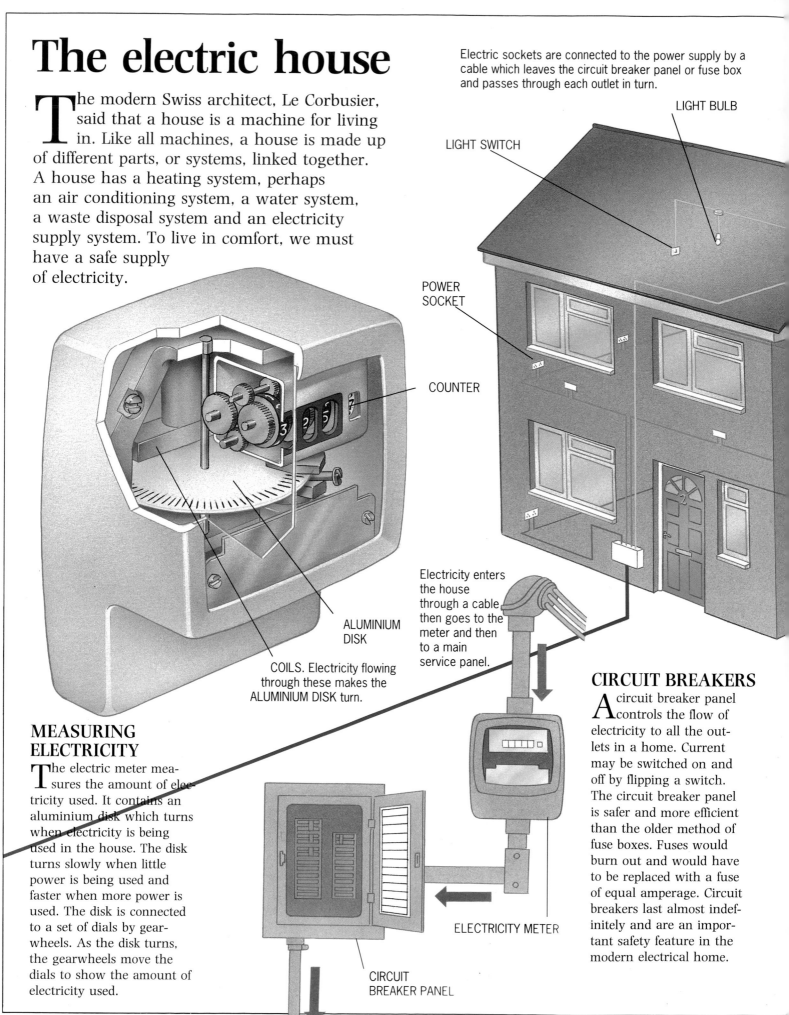

LIGHT BULB

LIGHT SWITCH

POWER SOCKET

COUNTER

ALUMINIUM DISK

COILS. Electricity flowing through these makes the ALUMINIUM DISK turn.

Electricity enters the house through a cable then goes to the meter and then to a main service panel.

ELECTRICITY METER

CIRCUIT BREAKER PANEL

MEASURING ELECTRICITY

The electric meter measures the amount of electricity used. It contains an aluminium disk which turns when electricity is being used in the house. The disk turns slowly when little power is being used and faster when more power is used. The disk is connected to a set of dials by gearwheels. As the disk turns, the gearwheels move the dials to show the amount of electricity used.

CIRCUIT BREAKERS

A circuit breaker panel controls the flow of electricity to all the outlets in a home. Current may be switched on and off by flipping a switch. The circuit breaker panel is safer and more efficient than the older method of fuse boxes. Fuses would burn out and would have to be replaced with a fuse of equal amperage. Circuit breakers last almost indefinitely and are an important safety feature in the modern electrical home.

ELECTRIC CIRCUITS

Electricity produced in power plants is supplied to our homes through a **service entrance cable**. Inside the house, the service entrance cable is connected to an electricity meter and a circuit breaker panel or fuse box. At the box, the wires branch into a number of different circuits, or electrical pathways. Power circuits supply electricity to the wall outlets and appliances, such as stoves. Other circuits, called lighting circuits, take power to the lights.

LIGHT BULB

LIGHT SWITCH

POWER SOCKET

LIVE WIRES

An electrical cable from an appliance has three separate wires, called the hot, neutral and ground wires. The hot and neutral wires form the electric circuit, linking the power supply to the appliance. The ground wire is a safety wire. It connects the body of the appliance to the earth and prevents the appliance from becoming "live".

CIRCUIT BREAKER

SAFETY FIRST

The circuit breaker is a safety device. If more electric current flows through the electric circuits than the circuit breaker is designed to carry, it switches off. This "breaks" the circuit and stops the flow of electricity before the wires can overheat and catch fire.

INSIDE A PLUG

Inside a plug, the hot, neutral and ground wires from the appliance cable are connected to the three pins. Each wire is wrapped in different colored plastic to identify it. A plastic bracket holds the electric cable tightly in place.

NEUTRAL WIRE

INSIDE AN OUTLET

When a plug is pushed into an electrical outlet, the plug pins come into contact with the hot, neutral and ground wires in the outlet. This completes the circuit between the appliance and the power supply.

HOT WIRE

GROUND WIRE

Electric power

The electric motor is the world's most common electrical machine. These motors are used in many different places in the home, factory and office. Anything that moves when the electricity is switched on contains an electric motor: food mixers, electric toothbrushes, sewing machines, and electric cars, for example. Electric motors come in many different sizes. The largest motors are as powerful as 1000 horses. The smallest electric motor of all was built in 1992 by Japanese engineers. It was just 0.8 mm across.

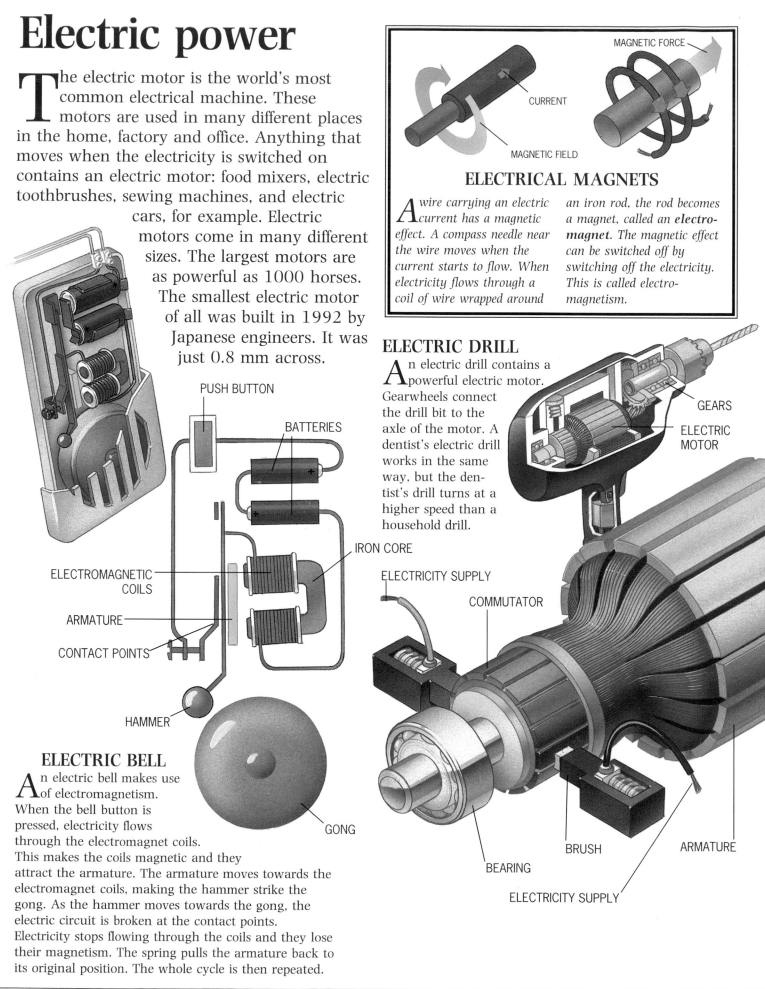

ELECTRICAL MAGNETS

CURRENT

MAGNETIC FIELD

MAGNETIC FORCE

A wire carrying an electric current has a magnetic effect. A compass needle near the wire moves when the current starts to flow. When electricity flows through a coil of wire wrapped around an iron rod, the rod becomes a magnet, called an **electromagnet**. The magnetic effect can be switched off by switching off the electricity. This is called electro-magnetism.

ELECTRIC DRILL

An electric drill contains a powerful electric motor. Gearwheels connect the drill bit to the axle of the motor. A dentist's electric drill works in the same way, but the dentist's drill turns at a higher speed than a household drill.

GEARS

ELECTRIC MOTOR

ELECTRICITY SUPPLY

COMMUTATOR

BEARING

BRUSH

ARMATURE

ELECTRICITY SUPPLY

PUSH BUTTON

BATTERIES

IRON CORE

ELECTROMAGNETIC COILS

ARMATURE

CONTACT POINTS

HAMMER

GONG

ELECTRIC BELL

An electric bell makes use of electromagnetism. When the bell button is pressed, electricity flows through the electromagnet coils. This makes the coils magnetic and they attract the armature. The armature moves towards the electromagnet coils, making the hammer strike the gong. As the hammer moves towards the gong, the electric circuit is broken at the contact points. Electricity stops flowing through the coils and they lose their magnetism. The spring pulls the armature back to its original position. The whole cycle is then repeated.

A simple electric motor consists of a coil of wire between the poles of a permanent magnet or electromagnet. The coil turns when an electric current flows through it. In larger motors, there is not just one coil but a series of coils, each being displaced by a small angle from the previous one.

FIELD COILS

BRISTLES

SWITCH

BATTERIES

COGWHEEL

ELECTRIC MOTOR

ELECTRIC TOOTHBRUSH

An electric toothbrush contains a small electric motor, powered by batteries in the handle. Gears and cogwheels make the bristles rotate. In some toothbrushes, each tuft of bristles revolves 42,000 times a minute, reversing direction 46 times each second.

BEARING

DRIVE SHAFT

ELECTRIC MOTOR

The motor shown here is a universal motor used in a clothes washing machine. It can run on **direct current** (DC) or on alternating current (AC). DC is the type of electricity produced by batteries. DC flows in one direction all the time. AC is the type of electricity produced by power stations. It reverses its direction of flow many times a second.

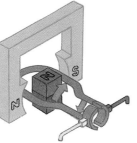
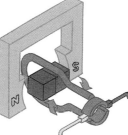

HOW AN ELECTRIC MOTOR WORKS

When electricity flows through the coil of a simple DC motor, the coil becomes magnetized. The north pole of the coil is attracted to the south pole of the **permanent magnet.**

The electric current is supplpied to the coil through a device called a commutator. The commutator consists of two half circles of metal attached to the ends of the coil.

The effect of the commutator is to reverse the direction of the current after the coil has made half a turn. If there was no commutator, the coil would come to rest after half a turn.

11

Keeping cool

Air conditioners, refrigerators and freezers have something in common with the sprays that dentists use to deaden our gums before an injection. The spray deadens the pain of the injection by rapidly cooling the gum, and 'freezing' it, as the spray evaporates. Inside a home freezer, the temperature can drop as low as –4 °F. Much lower temperatures are needed in a factory making frozen food. These low temperatures are achieved by evaporating liquids, too.

ELECTRIC REFRIGERATOR

In an electric refrigerator, an electric motor is used to pump a liquid, called a coolant, through pipes in the inner walls of the refrigerator. The coolant is a substance which evaporates easily to form a gas. When the coolant evaporates, it absorbs heat; when the gas condenses back to a liquid, it releases heat. The coolant is first compressed to a high pressure in the pipes at the back of the refrigerator. At this pressure, the coolant is a liquid. The compressed liquid is passed through a valve into the pipes inside the refrigerator. As this happens, the liquid evaporates rapidly, forming a gas. This fast evaporation absorbs heat from the inside of the refrigerator. The coolant gas is then pumped to the pipes at the back of the refrigerator. Here it is compressed again to turn it back into a liquid and reused.

GAS REFRIGERATOR

In a gas refrigerator, a small tank contains ammonia gas dissolved in water. The gas is released when the water is heated by a flame in a condenser and is then liquified. The cooled liquid is pumped to the inside of the refrigerator, where it evaporates back to a gas, absorbing heat.

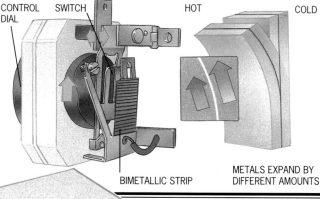

HOW A THERMOSTAT WORKS

The **thermostat** regulates the temperature in a refrigerator by turning the compressor motor on if the temperature rises. The thermostat contains a strip made of two layers of different metals joined together.

When the temperature rises, one metal expands more than the other. This causes the strip to bend and operate a switch. When the temperature drops, the strip unbends and the switch is turned off.

CONTROL DIAL

SWITCH

HOT

COLD

BIMETALLIC STRIP

METALS EXPAND BY DIFFERENT AMOUNTS

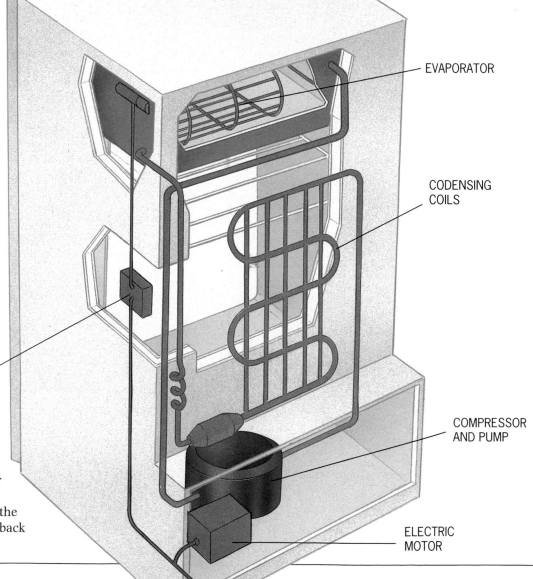

EVAPORATOR

CODENSING COILS

THERMOSTAT

COMPRESSOR AND PUMP

ELECTRIC MOTOR

AIR CONDITIONING

Air conditioning systems operate like electric refrigerators. An automobile air conditioning system, for example, has a compressor, condenser and evaporator. A coolant is compressed to a liquid and then pumped to the evaporator inside the car compartment, where it turns to a gas, absorbing heat. The heat is released at the condenser, outside the car compartment, when the gas changes back to a liquid. A room air conditioner pumps heat from a room in the same way.

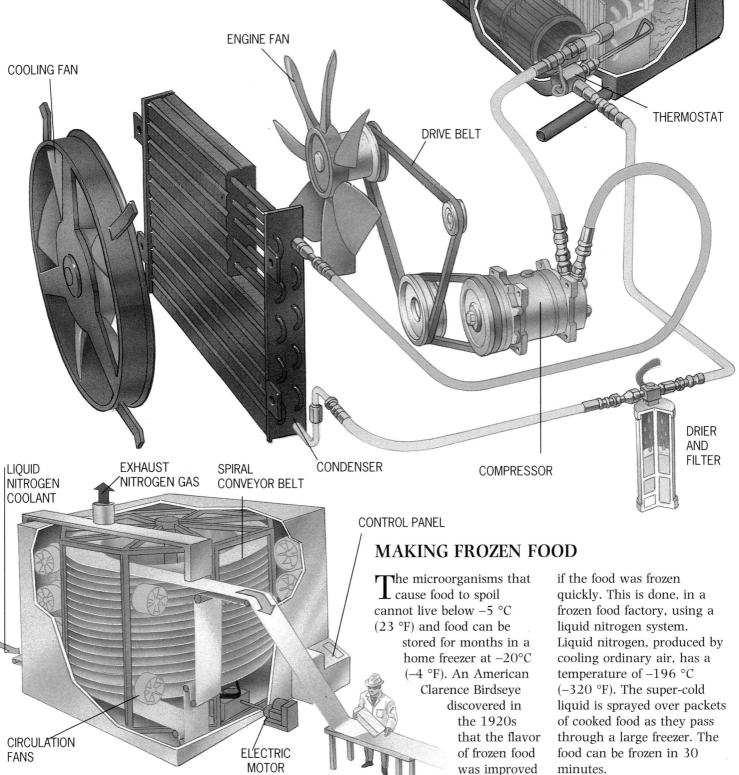

EVAPORATOR AND BLOWER

THERMOSTAT

ENGINE FAN

COOLING FAN

DRIVE BELT

DRIER AND FILTER

COOLING FAN

CONDENSER

COMPRESSOR

LIQUID NITROGEN COOLANT

EXHAUST NITROGEN GAS

SPIRAL CONVEYOR BELT

CONTROL PANEL

CIRCULATION FANS

ELECTRIC MOTOR

MAKING FROZEN FOOD

The microorganisms that cause food to spoil cannot live below −5 °C (23 °F) and food can be stored for months in a home freezer at −20°C (−4 °F). An American Clarence Birdseye discovered in the 1920s that the flavor of frozen food was improved if the food was frozen quickly. This is done, in a frozen food factory, using a liquid nitrogen system. Liquid nitrogen, produced by cooling ordinary air, has a temperature of −196 °C (−320 °F). The super-cold liquid is sprayed over packets of cooked food as they pass through a large freezer. The food can be frozen in 30 minutes.

Keeping warm

In one second the Sun gives off 13 million times more energy than all the electricity used in the USA in one year. In hot climates, this energy can be collected and used to heat homes and offices. In cold climates, we need to keep warm by burning fuels such as coal, wood and gas, or by using electricity. However we heat our homes, it is important not to waste heat.

CENTRAL HEATING

In cold climates, many houses have central heating. A boiler burns fuel, such as coal, gas or oil, to heat water. The hot water is pumped through pipes to radiators which heat the house. Some hot water is pumped to the hot water tank or cylinder.

EXPANSION TANK

HOT WATER CYLINDER

RADIATOR

PUMP

TEMPERATURE AND TIMECONTROLS

FIREBRICKS

AIR OUTLET

HEATING ELEMENTS

FAN

INSULATION

FAN HEATERS

Electric fan heaters are very efficient. Inside, coils of wire are heated as electricity flows through them. A fan blows air over the hot coils and into the room. Fan heaters usually have a built-in thermostat which switches off the electricity if the fan stops. Electric convector heaters rely on convection currents to carry heated air into the room.

STORAGE HEATER

In an electric storage heater, fire bricks enclose electric heating coils or elements. During the night, when electricity is cheaper, the coils heat the bricks. During the day, the bricks slowly give out the heat that they have absorbed during the night. If necessary, a fan blows air over the bricks to heat the room more quickly.

SWITCH

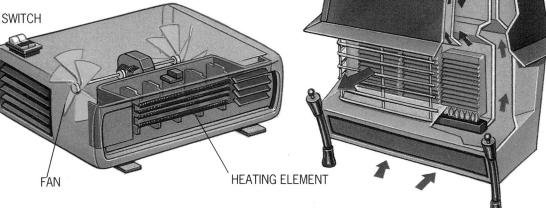

FAN

HEATING ELEMENT

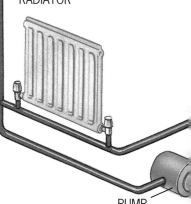

HOT WATER

Cold water flows into the bottom of the hot water cylinder. In the tank it is heated by a coiled pipe containing hot water. Then it flows to the hot water taps in the bathroom and kitchen.

BOILER

SOLAR HEATING

HEAT COLLECTOR

HOT WATER FROM COLLECTOR

COLD WATER TO HEAT COLLECTOR

INSULATION

Solar heaters collect the Sun's energy. The collector is a shallow box. The sides and back are painted black or covered with black plastic. The black surfaces absorb the Sun's heat. A glass sheet fitted over the collector prevents the heat escaping. The collector is like a car with closed windows in summer: it heats up quickly. Water is heated as it circulates through pipes in the collector. The warm water flows to a storage tank.

COLD WATER

BOILER

Cold water flows into the bottom of the boiler and hot water is pumped from the tank. A pipe leads from the boiler to an expansion tank in the loft so that if the water boils, steam escapes.

GAS FIRE

A gas fire heats a room by **conduction**, **convection** and **radiation**. The burning gas heats the ceramic grids at the front which give off radiant heat. The hot gases produced by the flames rise into the heat exchanger. Here they heat, by conduction, the air which has entered the heater at the bottom. The heated air flows through the grill at the top into the room, carrrying heat by convection.

VACUUM

CORK

DOUBLE-WALL GLASS BOTTLE

SILVERED SIDES

VACUUM FLASK

A **vacuum** flask or Thermos keeps hot drinks hot and cold drinks cold. It does this by stopping heat from traveling into or out of the flask. Some flasks consist of a double-walled glass bottle. Air is removed from between the walls, so that no heat can travel between the walls by conduction or convection. The walls are silvered to reflect heat rays.

METAL LAYER ON INSIDE OF INNER PANE

DRAFT-PROOF SEAL

OUTSIDE

20 MM AIR GAP

INSIDE

DESSICANT TO KEEP TRAPPED AIR DRY

DOUBLE GLAZING

Windows and doors that are double glazed keep heat in the house, so less heat is lost. The layer of air trapped between the panes acts as an **insulator**, or warm blanket of air separating the cold outer pane from the warmer inner pane.

Fire fighting

There have been many devasting fires throughout history. Rome was almost destroyed by fire in AD 62, London in 1666 and Chicago in 1871. The worst fire of all was in the Russian city of Moscow in 1571. More than 200,000 people died when the city was set alight by invaders. Small wonder that all cities now have fire departments, and homes and factories have fire alarms, sprinkler systems and fire extinguishers.

TELESCOPIC LADDER

RESCUE CRADLE

THE SIMON SNORKEL FIRE-FIGHTING TRUCK

FIRE ENGINE

The most common type of fire engine is called a pump escape. It has a powerful pump which can spray 1200 gallons of water each minute. Most modern fire engines have a hydraulically-powered ladder attached to a turntable. These ladders can be turned to any angle and extended to over 100 feet.

The ladder is used to help people escape from high windows, and to lift firefighters and hoses up. The engine also has tanks of water and fire-extinguishing foam.

There is equipment to break windows, lights, radio equipment and breathing apparatus. Despite their large size and weight, water pumps must be able to move quickly; they have a top speed of around 60 mph, and can reach 40 mph in less than 30 seconds.

Another type of fire engine is the foam truck used at airports. These machines have to deal with large oil fires that can start when aircraft crash. They pump out 6000 gallons of foam a minute from a range of 525 feet.

FOAM NOZZLE

SPRINKLER SYSTEM

A fire sprinkler system is a network of water-filled pipes crossing the ceiling of a factory or office. Glass bulbs attached to the pipes contain a liquid called acetate. If the temperature reaches a dangerous level, the acetate expands and releases water.

AIR BUBBLE

GLASS BULB

ACETATE LIQUID

WATER

DEFLECTOR PLATE

FIRE EXTINGUISHER

A fire extinguisher contains a substance - water, foam or powder - which can put out a fire. The fire-killing substance is forced out of the nozzle when the extinguisher is used. In a water extinguisher, the steel cylinder contains water and a cartridge of carbon dioxide at high pressure which forces the water through the nozzle when the operating lever is pressed.

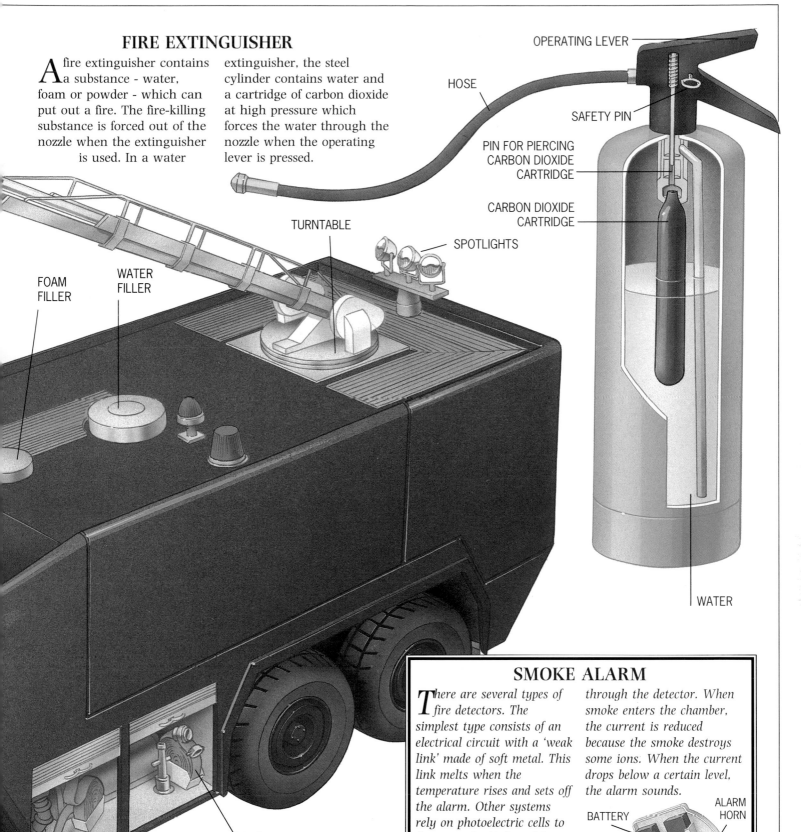

OPERATING LEVER

HOSE

SAFETY PIN

PIN FOR PIERCING
CARBON DIOXIDE
CARTRIDGE

CARBON DIOXIDE
CARTRIDGE

WATER

FOAM
FILLER

WATER
FILLER

TURNTABLE

SPOTLIGHTS

HOSES

SMOKE ALARM

*There are several types of fire detectors. The simplest type consists of an electrical circuit with a 'weak link' made of soft metal. This link melts when the temperature rises and sets off the alarm. Other systems rely on photoelectric cells to detect smoke. **Infrared** beams criss-cross the area. When a beam is interrupted by smoke, the alarm goes off. The ionization smoke detector has a chamber containing electrically-charged atoms (**ions**). The ions normally carry an electric current through the detector. When smoke enters the chamber, the current is reduced because the smoke destroys some ions. When the current drops below a certain level, the alarm sounds.*

BATTERY

ALARM
HORN

ESCAPE
LIGHT

IONIZATION
CHAMBER

Cooking

We all need to eat and drink. Even if we just have a slice of toast and a hot drink for breakfast, we use modern technology to prepare them. Modern electric or gas ovens, like the food processor, have made the cook's life much easier. Ovens can be programmed to switch on at any time, to set the required temperature, and switch off when the food is cooked. Even the electric kettle automatically turns itself off when the water in it boils.

COOKING BY MICROWAVES

A microwave oven bombards food with electromagnetic waves, called microwaves. The microwaves make the water molecules in the food vibrate, producing heat. The waves generate heat inside the food and so it cooks from the inside out, and more rapidly than in an ordinary oven. A device called a magnetron produces a beam of microwaves inside the oven. The beam falls on a spinning fan which reflects the microwaves onto the food from all angles. A turnable slowly rotates the food while it cooks to make sure it cooks evenly.

ELECTRIC OVEN

In the first electric ovens, made around 1880, food was heated by electricity passing through a wire wound around the cooking pot. In the 1890s, metal plates with wire underneath were used as heating elements. Modern heating elements which can be made in any shape came into use in the 1920s.

INSIDE THE OVEN

Heating elements inside an electric oven glow red hot when the oven is turned on. The temperature in the oven is controlled by a bimetallic strip or thermostat. This switches off the electricity supply to the elements when the right oven temperature is reached. Gas ovens often have rod thermostats. The oven temperature control is connected to a steel rod housed in a brass tube. The tube expands more than the rod when the oven heats up. This closes a valve which controls the flow of gas to the oven burners.

Heating elements on a hob consist of an inner conductor surrounded by an insulating layer with an outer metal covering. The electric current flows through the inner conductor heating the element.

MAGNETRON which produces the microwaves

MICROWAVE DEFLECTOR

GRILL HEATING ELEMENT

TURNTABLE which rotates the food

OVEN HEATING ELEMENT

PROCESSING FOOD

Afood processsor is used for shredding, slicing, mixing and liquefying food. It does this by spinning different-shaped blades at high speed. The processor is powered by an electric motor which spins at a speed of 15,000 revolutions per second. The liquefying blades are connected directly to the motor drive shaft and they rotate at the same high speed as the motor. The slicing and mixing blades are connected to the motor by a rubber belt and gears. The gears reduce the speed so that the blades rotate at a slower speed.

HEATING ELEMENT

OFF/ON SWITCH

MOTOR

DRIVE SHAFT

DRIVE BELT

ELECTRIC KETTLE

An electric kettle has a bimetallic strip thermostat in its handle. When the water boils, steam reaches the strip through a small hole. The heated strip bends and operates a switch which turns the electricity off.

TOASTING BREAD

When the bread-lowering handle of a toaster is pushed down, the bread moves between heating elements made of thin wires of nickel-chromium alloys woven between sheets of a mineral called mica. The bread is supported on a rack, which is held down by a catch. Lowering the bread switches on the electricity to the heating elements and they glow red hot. Near the heating elements is a timing device. It consists of a bimetallic strip which bends when it gets hot. When the strip has bent far enough, it touchs a plate (called the tripping plate) and completes an electric circuit. Electric current flows through the circuit, activating an electromagnet which releases the catch holding the bread rack down. The bread pops up, and the electricity is cut off.

HEATING ELEMENTS

MICA SHEETS

BROWNING CONTROL

BREAD LOWERING HANDLE

Cleaners

The clothes washer, dryer, steam iron and vacuum cleaner are essential items in any household. Yet it is relatively recently that these appliances were first sold. The first dishwasher was made in 1899. Dishes were stacked in a bowl and sprayed with water. The first vacuum cleaner was produced by Scottish inventor Herbert Booth in 1901. The first upright vacuum cleaner was designed in 1908. The first electric washing machines did not appear until 1914.

VACUUM CLEANER

In a vacuum cleaner, an electric motor spins a fan. The fan blows air out of the cleaner. This reduces the air pressure inside the cleaner. Air from outside the cleaner rushes in through the cleaning nozzle or attachment, carrying dust and dirt particles. Once inside the cleaner, the dirt-laden air flows into a cloth bag. The fabric of the bag traps the dirt and dust particles, but lets the air pass through its fibers. The clean air is blown out of the cleaner.

CLEANING UP

In an upright vacuum cleaner, the motor turns a roller at the front. The roller has rows of brushes and beater pads attached. The in-rushing air lifts the carpet while the beater pads loosen the dirt. The brushes lift off the dirt and it is sucked into the cleaner.

DUST PARTICLES trapped in bag

BRUSHES to loosen dirt on carpet

AIR being sucked into cleaner

INLET TUBE

DISPOSABLE DUST BAG

FAN

ELECTRIC MOTOR

CONTROL
PANEL

SOAP CONTAINER

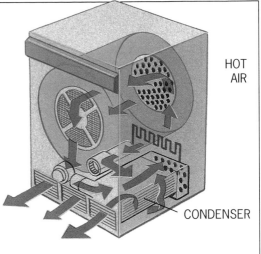

HOT
AIR

GLASS
DOOR

WATER
INLET

FILTER

WATER
OUTLET

CONDENSER

MOTOR

TUMBLE DRYER

Hot air circulates around the clothes in a tumble dryer, as the drum rotates. Ribs in the drum lift the clothes to the top of the drum and they fall through the hot air. Moisture in the clothes is absorbed by the air. The air then passes through a filter which removes dust. A condenser removes the moisture.

CLOTHES WASHER

Like many household appliances, clothes washers and dryers rely on electric motors and heating elements. In a washing machine, water flows into the cylinder which holds the dirty clothes through the soap box, mixing in the soap. The water may then be heated by the heating element. The cylinder is turned to wash the clothes, and water pumped in and out as the wash and rinse proceeds. The washing cycle is controlled by the electronic circuits in the control panel. The temperature of the water and length of the wash are all automatically controlled.

STEAM IRON

In a steam iron, a metal plate, called the sole plate, is heated when electricity flows through a heating element. A thermostat controls the temperature of the sole plate by switching the electricity off and on. Steam is produced when water drips from a small tank, inside the iron, onto the top of the heated plate. The steam then passes through holes in the plate, and onto the clothes. Some irons have a small piston which produces a powerful surge of steam when the steam control button is pressed.

STEAM CONTROL BUTTON

WATER
TANK

THE THERMOSTAT

The thermostat in a steam iron is a bimetallic strip connected to the heating element and power.

ELEMENT

POWER
SUPPLY

BIMETALLIC STRIP

ELEMENT

POWER
SUPPLY

When the bimetallic strip heats up, it bends, breaking the electrical circuit and the iron cools.

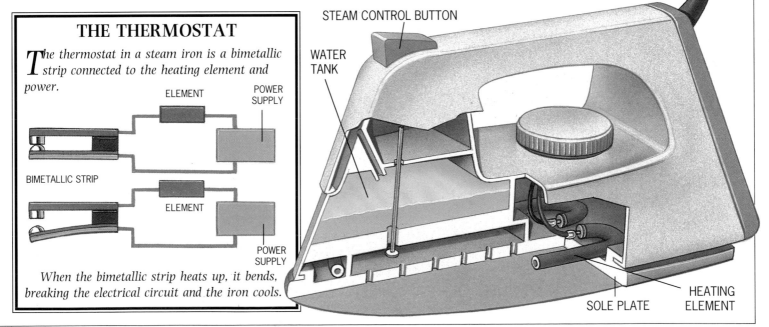

SOLE PLATE

HEATING
ELEMENT

In the garden

Let's get the work done, so we can have some fun! There are many tools that can make work in the garden easier. Some of these tools are simple. Hedge trimmers and pruning shears are like scissors used to cut paper. A lawn sprinkler is just as simple. Other garden tools are more complicated. The hover mower is like a hovercraft, a type of aircraft. A hedge trimmer is like a barber's haircutter, with blades that move back and forth.

TYPES OF MOWERS

There are several different mower types. Cylinder mowers have a rotating cutting cylinder with a series of blades wrapped around the cylinder. The grass is cut by a scissor action between the cylinder blades and a fixed bottom blade. Rotary mowers have a single rotating blade enclosed in a casing on wheels.

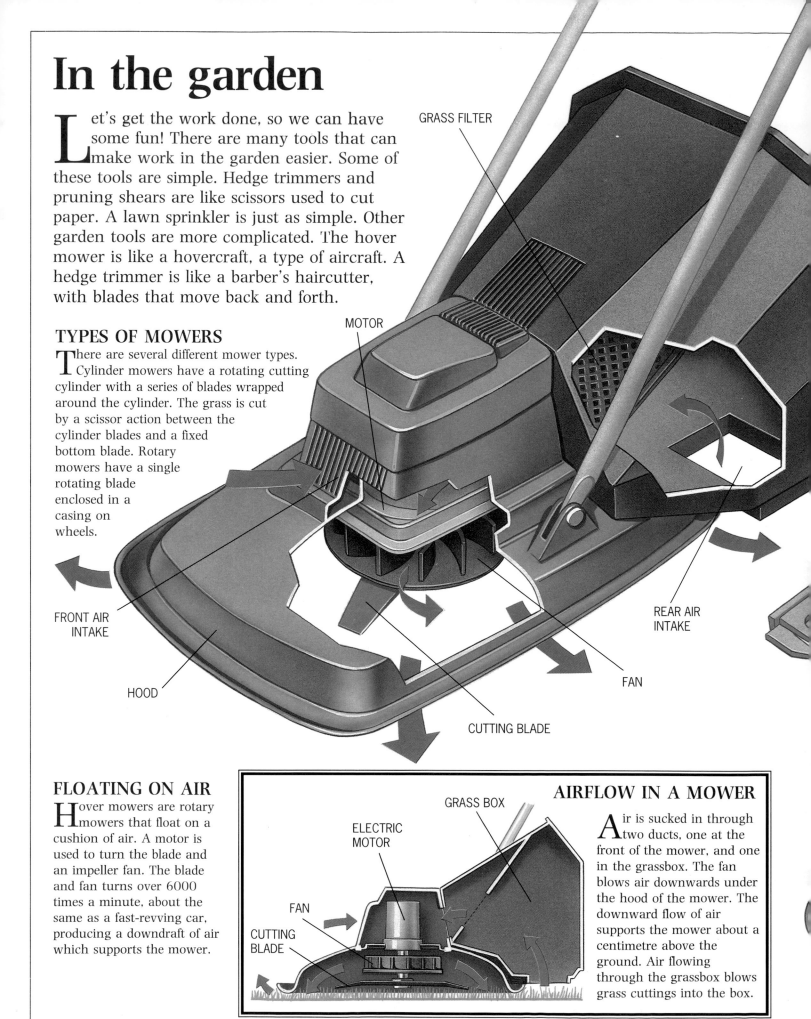

GRASS FILTER

MOTOR

FRONT AIR INTAKE

HOOD

CUTTING BLADE

FAN

REAR AIR INTAKE

FLOATING ON AIR

Hover mowers are rotary mowers that float on a cushion of air. A motor is used to turn the blade and an impeller fan. The blade and fan turns over 6000 times a minute, about the same as a fast-revving car, producing a downdraft of air which supports the mower.

ELECTRIC MOTOR

GRASS BOX

FAN

CUTTING BLADE

AIRFLOW IN A MOWER

Air is sucked in through two ducts, one at the front of the mower, and one in the grassbox. The fan blows air downwards under the hood of the mower. The downward flow of air supports the mower about a centimetre above the ground. Air flowing through the grassbox blows grass cuttings into the box.

HEDGE TRIMMER

Ahedge trimmer is sometimes powered by electricity. An electric motor inside turns when the power is turned on. In order to make the cutting blades move back and forth, a combination of **gears** and **cranks** is used. The crank is a wheel to which the blades are attached by a pivoted rod. The blades move back and forth as the wheel turns. The gears (toothed wheels) link the motor to the crank wheel.

GRASS BOX

ONE BLADE MOVES
BACK AND FORTH

SPRINKLERS

Sprinklers cannot work without a high water pressure to force the water through the tiny holes. The water emerges as a fine spray of droplets which travels a long distance. Sprinklers which spin around do so because the emerging water pushes backwards on the sprinkler arms. Other sprinklers have built-in gears which turn the spray arm.

LEVERS IN THE GARDEN

Hedge trimmers and branch cutters are joined pairs of levers. A lever can magnify a force if it is long enough. This is why garden tools often have long handles.

Grass shears don't need to exert a great force, so they have short handles. They have long blades instead, so that cutting is quicker.

Pruning shears can exert great force if the branch to be cut is close to the blade pivot. The force exerted increases if the cutter has long handles.

At play

Let's have fun! Not all machines are made to do work. The bumper car and the jet ski are fun machines. But these machines are as interesting to study as, say, a food processor or jet engine. In fact, a food processor is a lot like a bumper car: both devices are basically electric motors. The jet ski is just a jet engine that works in water, instead of air.

WATER MOTORCYCLE

A jet ski looks like a motorcycle on water. In calm weather it can race along at 40 mph. The driver stands or kneels on the craft and steers by using handlebars like a motorcycle's. The ski is powered by a small internal combustion engine, like a motorcycle. The engine powers an impeller or water jet, not a propeller. A jet ski is self-righting; if it should turn over, it automatically turns itself upright again. Also, if the rider falls off, the ski automatically circles, returning to the rider.

BUMPER CARS

Bumper cars, popular at the fairground, are really just moving parts of an electric circuit. The metal floor on which they run is one part of the circuit. The floor is connected to one terminal of an electrical generator. The ceiling is a wire mesh. This is connected to the other terminal of the generator. The bumper car completes the circuit. A flexible metal strip, called the pillar, rises from the top of the car and presses against the ceiling mesh. When the rider presses the foot pedal, the circuit between the ceiling and floor is completed. Electricity flows through the electric motor in the car, and the car moves along.

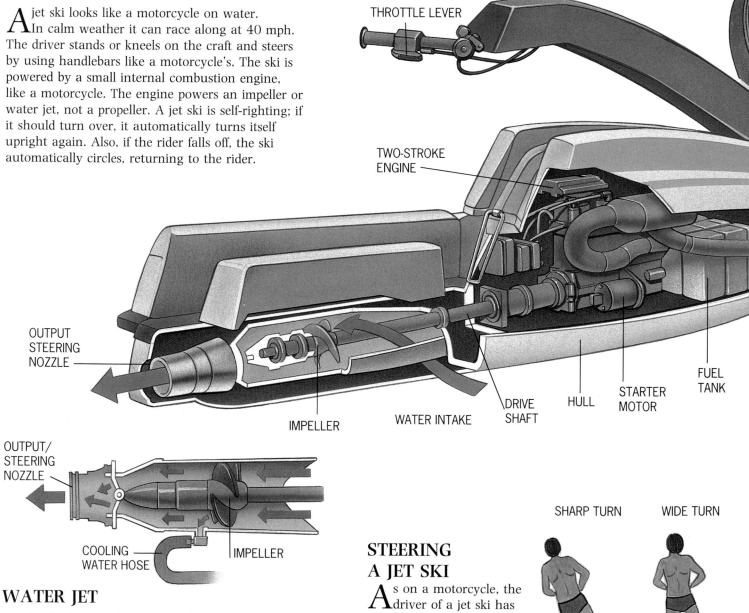

THROTTLE LEVER

TWO-STROKE ENGINE

OUTPUT STEERING NOZZLE

IMPELLER

WATER INTAKE

DRIVE SHAFT

HULL

STARTER MOTOR

FUEL TANK

OUTPUT/ STEERING NOZZLE

COOLING WATER HOSE

IMPELLER

WATER JET

A jet ski does not have a propeller. Instead it has an impeller which works like a jet engine. The impeller sucks in water through an intake nozzle under the craft. The water is expelled at high speed through a nozzle at the back. This drives the ski forward. Changing the direction of the back nozzle is used to steer the ski.

STEERING A JET SKI

As on a motorcycle, the driver of a jet ski has to lean sideways when making a turn. This maintains the balance. The higher the speed or the tighter the turn, the more the driver has to lean.

SHARP TURN   WIDE TURN

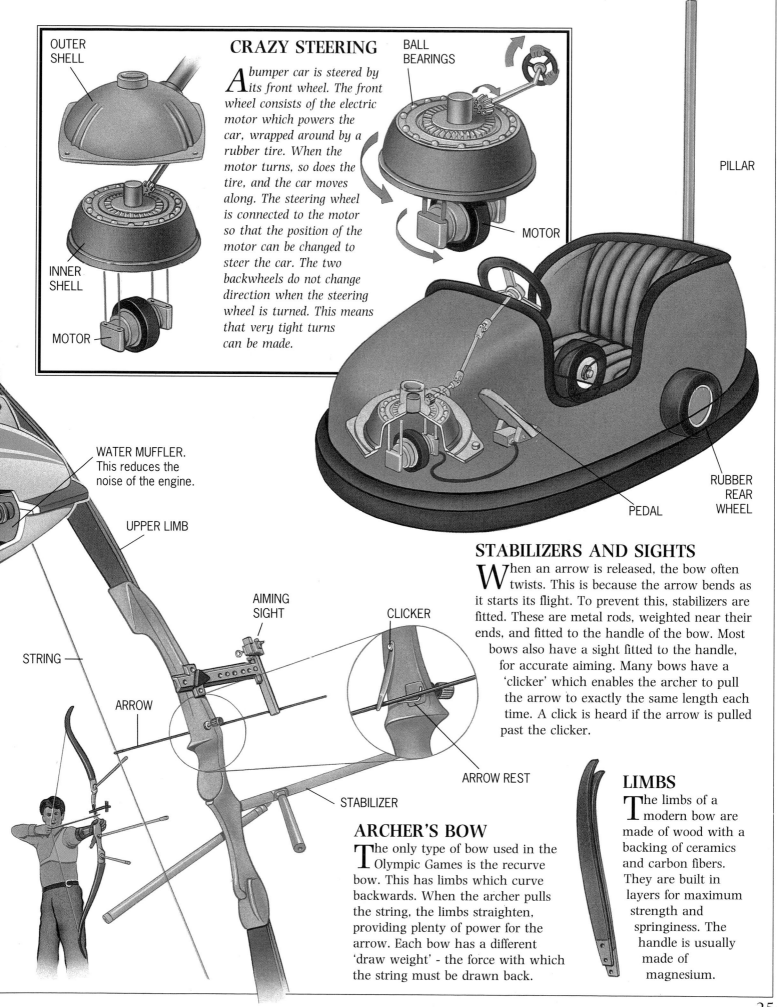

OUTER
SHELL

INNER
SHELL

MOTOR

CRAZY STEERING

A bumper car is steered by its front wheel. The front wheel consists of the electric motor which powers the car, wrapped around by a rubber tire. When the motor turns, so does the tire, and the car moves along. The steering wheel is connected to the motor so that the position of the motor can be changed to steer the car. The two backwheels do not change direction when the steering wheel is turned. This means that very tight turns can be made.

BALL
BEARINGS

MOTOR

PILLAR

RUBBER
REAR
WHEEL

PEDAL

WATER MUFFLER.
This reduces the
noise of the engine.

UPPER LIMB

AIMING
SIGHT

CLICKER

STRING

ARROW

ARROW REST

STABILIZER

STABILIZERS AND SIGHTS

When an arrow is released, the bow often twists. This is because the arrow bends as it starts its flight. To prevent this, stabilizers are fitted. These are metal rods, weighted near their ends, and fitted to the handle of the bow. Most bows also have a sight fitted to the handle, for accurate aiming. Many bows have a 'clicker' which enables the archer to pull the arrow to exactly the same length each time. A click is heard if the arrow is pulled past the clicker.

ARCHER'S BOW

The only type of bow used in the Olympic Games is the recurve bow. This has limbs which curve backwards. When the archer pulls the string, the limbs straighten, providing plenty of power for the arrow. Each bow has a different 'draw weight' - the force with which the string must be drawn back.

LIMBS

The limbs of a modern bow are made of wood with a backing of ceramics and carbon fibers. They are built in layers for maximum strength and springiness. The handle is usually made of magnesium.

Musical instruments

There are several families, or types, of musical instruments. A drum is called a percussion instrument, an instrument that is struck to make a sound. Instruments in which the musician blows into a hollow reed are called wind instruments. A string instrument makes a sound when a string is struck or stroked. A brass instrument is a metal tube with a mouthpiece at one end and a bell-like flare at the other.

WIND INSTRUMENT

A church organ is a wind instrument, like the flute, piccolo, recorder, clarinet, oboe and bassoon. Notes are produced by blowing air into pipes of different lengths. The pitch of the notes produced depends on the lengths of the pipes being blown.

THE STOPS

The stops, or knobs, near the keyboards control the air flow to each rank of pipes. For instance, if a particular stop is pulled out, a perforated slider moves beneath openings of some of the pipes. Pressing a note on the keyboard will allow air to flow only to those pipes near the holes in the stop. This means that many different combinations of notes can be sounded at once, by pulling different stops.

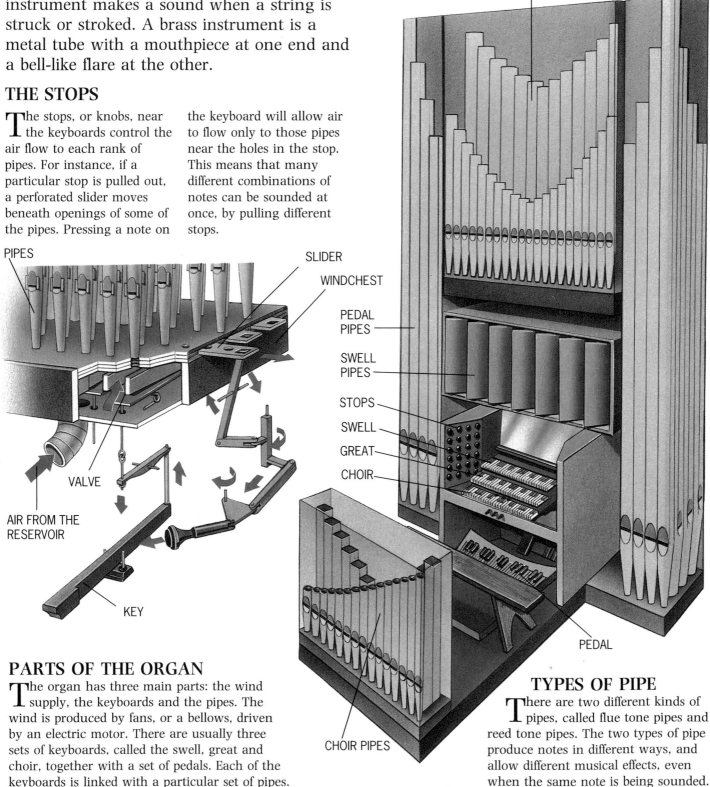

PIPES

SLIDER

WINDCHEST

VALVE

AIR FROM THE
RESERVOIR

KEY

GREAT PIPES

PEDAL
PIPES

SWELL
PIPES

STOPS

SWELL

GREAT

CHOIR

PEDAL

CHOIR PIPES

PARTS OF THE ORGAN

The organ has three main parts: the wind supply, the keyboards and the pipes. The wind is produced by fans, or a bellows, driven by an electric motor. There are usually three sets of keyboards, called the swell, great and choir, together with a set of pedals. Each of the keyboards is linked with a particular set of pipes.

TYPES OF PIPE

There are two different kinds of pipes, called flue tone pipes and reed tone pipes. The two types of pipe produce notes in different ways, and allow different musical effects, even when the same note is being sounded.

STRING INSTRUMENT

The violin is a string instrument, like the viola, cello, double bass, guitar, and banjo. A stretched string, plucked in the middle, will vibrate at a frequency which depends upon the length of the string, its thickness, and how tightly it is stretched.

A violin player, for example, can change the pitch of a string by moving a finger along the neck of the violin, altering the length of the sounding string. Some string instruments, such as guitars and mandolins, have frets (small metal strips) across the fingerboard at certain points.

The pitch can be altered by tightening the string, as when the string is tuned. And, the heavy bass strings naturally produce lower notes than the lighter strings.

FINGERBOARD

STRINGS

BRIDGE

TAIL PIECE

CHINREST

NECK

TOP PLATE

TUNING PEG

BASS BAR

F HOLE

END BUTTON

BACK PLATE

PIANO

Keyboard instruments, such as the piano, are often classed with percussion instruments. A piano has strings which sound when they are struck by a hammer when a key is pressed. The piano can produce more notes than any other musical instrument. A piano can produce a note twice as high as the highest note of a violin, and its lowest note is ten times lower than the lowest note of a violin. As well as its natural pitch, a musical instrument produces other weaker notes, called overtones or harmonics. Each instrument produces its own characteristic mixture of harmonics. This is why the different instruments sound different, even if sounding the same note.

HOW A PIANO KEY WORKS

Each key in a piano is linked to a felt-tipped hammer by a complicated series of levers, called the 'action'. The levers magnify the movements of the keys so that the hammer moves faster than the key. This means that the hammer can strike a string and move away quickly, allowing short notes to be played. The hammer is caught by a device called a backcheck on its return, preventing a rebound. Another device, the damper, stops the string sounding when a key is released.

FELT HAMMER

LEVER TO MOVE HAMMER

KEY

STRINGS. A modern grand piano has 230 strings which exert a force of 20 tons on the iron frame.

IRON FRAME

KEYBOARD

On your bike

The modern bicycle is the most efficient machine ever made. It uses less energy in traveling a given distance than any other machine, or animal. A cyclist can travel 1,500 miles on the food energy equivalent of about a gallon of gasoline. This is far more economic than a car, which does about 25 miles per gallon. No wonder more than 100 million cycles are made worldwide each year.

THE GREEN MACHINE

Eight-tenths of the pedaled energy is transmitted to the rear wheel of a bike. By contrast, a car wastes most of its energy fighting friction or producing noise and waste heat. Whereas a car produces over four times its own weight in fumes each year, a bike produces none. For these reasons, it is sometimes called the 'green machine'.

THE LOW RIDER

The most efficient bikes of all are called recumbents. In these, the rider is lying down, with legs pointing forwards. In some recumbents, the rider is lying almost flat. These machines slip through the air very easily. There is little air resistance, and it takes less energy to keep a recumbent moving at speed. It takes about one-fifth less power to maintain cruising speed on a recumbent than on a normal bike.

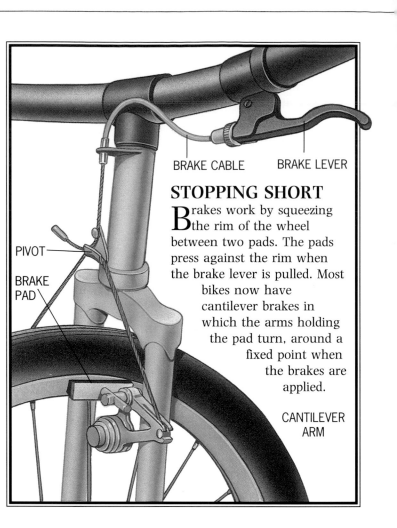

BRAKE CABLE   BRAKE LEVER

STOPPING SHORT

Brakes work by squeezing the rim of the wheel between two pads. The pads press against the rim when the brake lever is pulled. Most bikes now have cantilever brakes in which the arms holding the pad turn, around a fixed point when the brakes are applied.

PIVOT

BRAKE PAD

CANTILEVER ARM

BICYCLE FACTS

◆ A recently-discovered drawing by famous Italian inventor and artist Leonardo da Vinci shows a design for a bike, drawn in about 1490, with all the features of a modern machine. There is no evidence that the bike was ever built.
◆ In 1881, there were only five cycles in Moscow, yet police were sufficiently worried that they banned riding in the city.
◆ The smallest bike of all time has wheels of $1/2$ inch across. It was made by Neville Patten of Australia, and ridden by him a distance of $13 1/2$ feet in 1988.

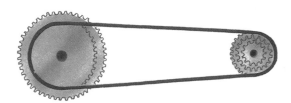

The rear cogwheel is the same size as the pedal wheel - just right for going up hills!

HOW A DYNAMO WORKS

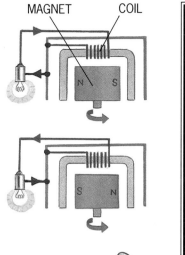

MAGNET   COIL

As the magnet in a dynamo turns it produces (or 'induces') an electric current in the coil. This effect, called electromagnetic induction, was discovered by English scientist Michael Faraday in the 1830s.

A dynamo consists of a cylindrical magnet inside an iron core. A toothed wheel attached to the top of the magnet grips the bicycle tire and spins the magnet when the wheel turns. A coil of wire is wound around the bottom of the core. The electric current produced flows through a single wire from the coil to the lamp.

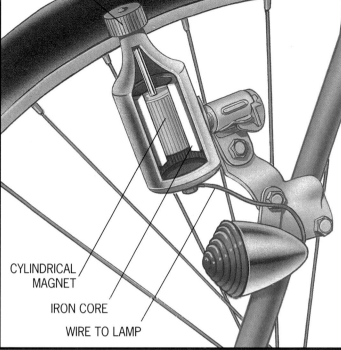

TOOTHED WHEEL

CYLINDRICAL MAGNET

IRON CORE

WIRE TO LAMP

GEAR WHEELS

IN GEAR

The pedal wheel of a bike is connected to the back wheel by a chain. Teeth on the wheels fit into the chain. There are more teeth on the pedal wheel than the back wheel. This means that if the pedal wheel makes one turn, the back wheel makes more than one turn. This is called 'gearing'. Some bicycles have more than one gear, which means that the the number of teeth on the rear wheel can be changed.

The rear cogwheel is smaller than the pedal wheel - just right for going fast!

The derailleur gear system has several cogwheels attached to the rear wheel. The chain is moved to a different cogwheel when the gears are changed.

29

See near and far

Looking up at the night sky, you can see objects - stars, of course - millions of miles away. But your eyes have limitations. There are stars that are too faint to see. There are also tiny organisms, such as bacteria, that are too small to be seen with the unaided eye. We must rely on optical instruments - the telescope, camera, microscope - to see these things.

HOW LENSES WORK

Most optical instruments use lenses. A **convex lens** is a piece of transparent material bulging outwards on both sides. When a small object is held near a convex lens, the light rays from the object are bent as they pass through the glass. The rays are bent so that they converge or come closer together. This produces a magnified image, or picture, of the object. A concave lens has inward-curving surfaces. Light rays are made to diverge, or spread, by a concave lens.

CONVEX LENS

CONCAVE LENS

TERRESTRIAL TELESCOPE

EYEPIECE LENS

LENS TELESCOPE

All telescopes have two main parts; the **objective**, which may be a curved mirror or a large lens, and the eyepiece, consisting of a lens or group of lenses. The objective forms an image (or picture) of a distant object, and this image is magnified by the eyepiece. The telescope is focused by moving the eyepiece backwards and forwards until the image becomes clear. Some telescopes have a convex lens objective and a concave lens eyepiece; this combination produces an upright image. Astronomer's lens telescopes have convex lenses for both objective and eyepiece; this produces an upside-down image - which, of course, doesn't matter when you are looking at stars.

SHUTTER SPEED ADJUSTMENT

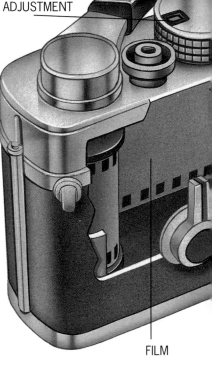

FILM

SHUTTER. Shutter speed determines how moving subjects are captured. Fast shutter speeds 'freeze' fast action, which our eyes would see as a blur.

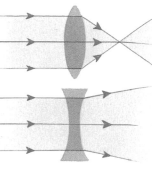

EYEPIECE LENS

PRISMS

OBJECTIVE LENS

BINOCULARS

Binoculars are really a pair of telescopes - one for each eye. The telescopes are made shorter so that the binoculars are easier to handle. This is achieved by using a pair of right-angled prisms. The prisms fold the light as it travels through the binoculars. This not only makes the instrument shorter but the prisms also turn the image right way up.

THE MECHANICAL EYE

A camera is the mechanical equivalent of our eye. It is a simple device - a box with a hole and lens at one end, and a light-sensitive film at the other. Light enters the camera through the hole, called the aperture, when a shutter opens. An image is formed on the film. The film is then developed, or treated chemically, and the image made visible and fixed. Each part of a camera can be adjusted. The shutter speed, the aperture size, the film sensitivity, and the lens, can all be changed. The telephoto lens (right) is like a small telescope which can be attached to a camera.

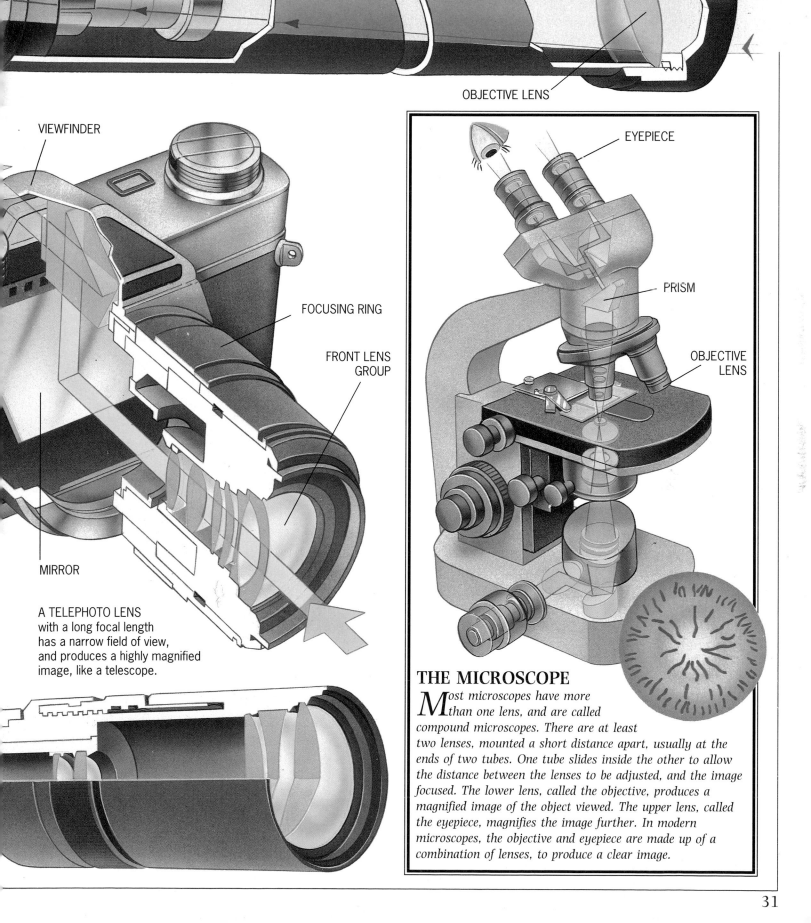

OBJECTIVE LENS

VIEWFINDER

FOCUSING RING

FRONT LENS GROUP

EYEPIECE

PRISM

OBJECTIVE LENS

MIRROR

A TELEPHOTO LENS with a long focal length has a narrow field of view, and produces a highly magnified image, like a telescope.

THE MICROSCOPE

*M*ost microscopes have more than one lens, and are called compound microscopes. There are at least two lenses, mounted a short distance apart, usually at the ends of two tubes. One tube slides inside the other to allow the distance between the lenses to be adjusted, and the image focused. The lower lens, called the objective, produces a magnified image of the object viewed. The upper lens, called the eyepiece, magnifies the image further. In modern microscopes, the objective and eyepiece are made up of a combination of lenses, to produce a clear image.

Computers

A computer is sometimes called an 'electronic brain'. Yet a computer is not a brain. It is merely an electronic device that can remember facts and calculate very fast, making thousands or millions of calculations each second. In fact, a computer is not 'brainy' or intelligent at all; it needs detailed instructions before it can perform even the simplest task. The instructions, called the program, have to be given to the computer by its human user.

SILICON CHIP, with complicated electronic circuit etched on.

SILICON CHIPS

Silicon chips, also called integrated circuits, are the building blocks of modern computers. Each silicon chip contains a complete electronic circuit etched onto a small piece of silicon, the size of a child's fingernail. There are many different types of chip, each with a different job to do. The microprocessor chip does all the calculations and controls the operation of the computer. Memory chips, store information inside the computer.

CASING or container to make the chip easier to handle. The chip is connected to the legs or pins by gold wires.

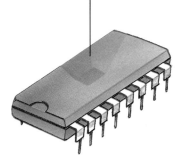

ON/OFF SWITCH

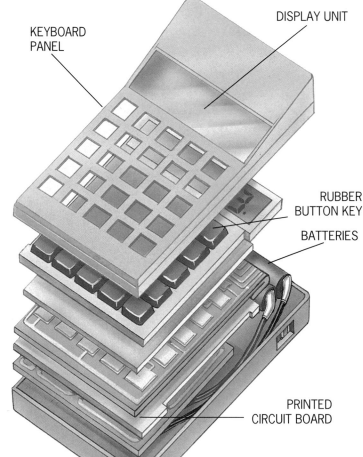

KEYBOARD PANEL

DISPLAY UNIT

RUBBER BUTTON KEY

BATTERIES

PRINTED CIRCUIT BOARD

MOUSE

KEYBOARD

INSIDE A CALCULATOR

Like a computer, a calculator is made up of input, output, memory and processing units. Most of the space inside a calculator is taken by the display panel (output), keyboard (input) and casing. The integrated circuit which provides the memory and processing takes up little space.

THE MOUSE

A mouse is a hand-held input device which allows you to control the movement of a pointer on the computer screen. You can make selections and give instructions by moving the pointer to a symbol on the screen and pressing a button on the mouse. The mouse contains a rubber-coated ball that rolls when the mouse is moved. As the ball rolls, detectors register the motion and move the pointer on the screen.

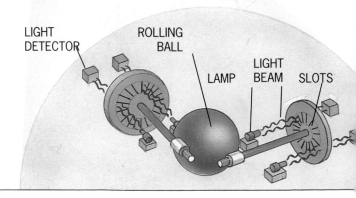

LIGHT DETECTOR

ROLLING BALL

LAMP

LIGHT BEAM

SLOTS

INSIDE A COMPUTER

There are four main parts to a computer. The first is the input device used to give information and instructions to the computer. The most common input device is a keyboard, like a typewriter keyboard. Secondly, there is an output device. This shows the results of the computer's work - it can be a video screen or a printer. Thirdly, there is the computer's memory. One type of memory device is called a **floppy disk**. This is like a small bendy music record.

The final part of a computer is its processing unit. This is the part of the computer, containing the **microprocessor**, which receives the program instructions, does the calculations, and tells the output screen to display the answers.

INPUT / OUTPUT
CONTROLLERS

MONITOR

VIDEO CONTROLLER

MICROPROCESSOR

MEMORY
CHIPS

HARD DISK

FLOPPY DISK

NUMBER, or NUMERIC,
KEYS, for calculations

FLOPPY DISKS

Floppy disks hold information (called data, in computer jargon) or program instructions. The thin plastic floppy disks are inserted into the drive unit to read or write information. The data is stored as a magnetic pattern on the disk and is read or written by a magnetic head inside the drive unit.

THE KEYBOARD

The keyboard is really a set of switches, one for each key. When you press a key you close the switch for that key and send a signal to the computer. The computer is continuously checking the keyboard and can work out which key has been pressed from the signal.

HARD DISKS

Some computers have a built-in hard disk memory. Like floppy disk units, these store information as a magnetic pattern on a plate-shaped disk. The disks are called 'hard' because they are made of metal and are rigid. A hard disk unit has several disks and so can store more information than a single floppy disk.

Radio

Radio waves are 'ripples' of electricity and magnetism which travel through space at the speed of light. The waves - called electromagnetic waves - spread out from a radio station, carrying a signal. When the wave passes over a radio antenna, the electronic circuit in the radio detects the wave and feeds the signal carried by the wave to the loudspeaker. The loudspeaker converts the signal to speech or music.

WAVELENGTH

The wavelength of a radio wave is the distance between two successive peaks in the wave. Radio waves can have wavelengths as small as 1 mm ($^4/_{100}$ inch) or be over 1 mile long.

PEAK   WAVELENGTH

TROUGH

MICROPHONE

There are a number of different kinds of microphones. The most widely used is the moving coil microphone. Sound waves strike the cone, or diaphragm, making it vibrate. The cone is attached to a coil of wire which moves between the poles of an electro-magnet producing an electrical signal.

CONE

COIL

MAGNET

ANTENNA for short wave transmission

HIGH-FREQUENCY AMPLIFICATION CIRCUIT

BATTERIES

WAVELENGTHS

There are five different wavelengths in use: long wave, medium wave, ultra-short wave (also called FM) and microwave.

MODULATION

Making a radio wave carry a signal is called **modulation**. The radio station sends out a steady radio wave, called the **carrier wave**. In the station, a microphone turns the sound into an electrical signal which is mixed with the carrier wave. There are two main systems of modulation, called amplitude modulation (AM) and **frequency** modulation or FM.

LOUDSPEAKER

A moving-coil loudspeaker works in the reverse way to a moving-coil microphone. Varying electrical signals pass through the coil, making it vibrate. The vibration of the coil is passed to the paper cone of the speaker, which also vibrates, producing sounds.

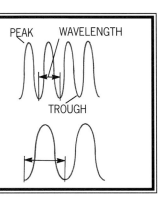

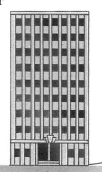

ANTENNA

A radio antenna is the 'doorway' into the radio. Since many different radio waves fall on the antenna, the radio must be tuned to the correct frequency.

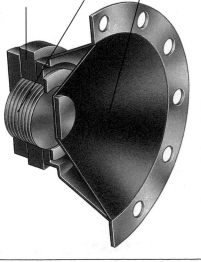

CIRCULAR MAGNET   COIL   CONE

FERRITE BAR ANTENNA for
long and medium waves

MAIN CIRCUIT BOARD
holding integrated circuits

LOUDSPEAKER

DEMODULATION

The next stage is **demodulation** - this is the reverse of modulation. The carrier wave and the signal are separated. Because there are two separate methods of modulation (AM and FM) there are separate FM and AM demodulation sections.

FREQUENCY DISPLAY

HIGH-FREQUENCY AMPLIFIER

The signal received by the antenna is very weak and must be strengthened, or amplified, before it can pass to the other radio sections. This is done by a 'high frequency' amplifier, which boosts its strength by 10 times.

TUNING BUTTONS

MORE AMPLIFIERS

There are also extra low-frequency amplifiers to boost the signal. By the time the signal is fed to the loudspeaker, it has been amplified to over 10,000 times its original strength. Only then is it strong enough to work the speakers.

RADIO CONTROL

The simplest radio controlled models are called 'single channel' models. The operator is only able to control one aspect of the model's behavior. In a model aircraft, for example, *the steering or rudder is often controlled by the transmitted signal. In more complicated 'multi-channel' systems, the model can be controlled more accurately using a joystick like the control column of a real aircraft.*

Television & video

The word 'television' means 'pictures from far away'. And television picture can be sent truly astronomical distances. On 25 August 1989, the Voyager 2 spaceprobe sent back to Earth television pictures of the planet Neptune, nearly three billion miles away. By the time the signal had reached the Earth, its strength was 20,000 million times weaker than the current from a tiny watch battery. Yet this tiny signal was sufficient to carry to Earth breathtaking views of the distant planet.

MAKING PICTURES

The screen of a television set is one end of a glass tube called a **cathode ray tube**. The inside of the tube is coated inside with chemicals called **phosphors**. These phosphors glow when they are hit by electrons (electrical particles). At the back end of the television tube is an **electron** gun. The gun produces electrons and shoots them towards the screen. The beam of electrons zigzags across the screen - at a speed of nearly 22,000 mph - in horizontal lines. As the beam moves across the screen, the glow produced forms the picture. Every second 25 or 30 separate pictures are displayed.

SHADOWMASK

PHOSPHOR DOTS

SCREEN

ELECTRON GUNS

ELECTRON BEAMS

HOLES IN SHADOWMASK

CATHODE RAY TUBE

ELECTRON GUNS

MAIN CIRCUIT BOARD

ELECTRON GUNS

The signal received from the aerial contains three parts corresponding to the different colors in the transmitted picture. These parts are fed to separate electron guns in the cathode ray tube.

SHADOWMASK

The electron beams, one for each color (red, blue, green), pass through a plate called a shadow mask just behind the screen. This contains half a million small holes, aligned so that each electron beam only hits the dots that glow in the correct color.

DOTTYVISION

In a color television set, the phosphors are coated on the screen in a pattern of three dots, one dot that glows red, one blue and one green. At any spot on the screen, the three colors combine to match the colors of the original picture.

INFRARED RAYS

SHADOWMASK

LOUDSPEAKER

REMOTE CONTROL UNIT

A remote control unit uses infrared rays - heat rays - to control the television. The infrared rays are transmitted by the hand-held unit, and are detected by a receiver unit at the front of the television.

VIDEO RECORDER

Video recorders store pictures on magnetic tape, similar to the magnetic tapes used to record music, except that video tapes are wider than music tapes. The signal on a video tape is recorded in a diagonal pattern across the tape. This enables more information to be held on a tape.

VIDEOTAPE ARRANGEMENT

The record and replay head of a video recorder is more complicated than the head of a sound tape machine. There are two heads inside a drum which turns as the tape moves across it. The drum is tilted so that the heads produce a sloping pattern of magnetism when they record on the tape.

CABLE TV

Most homes receive a television signal through a cable that provides many more channels than using an antenna. Local cable companies wire homes and charge a monthly fee to use their service.

ANTENNA

Like a radio receiver, a television set has an antenna, which picks up the electromagnetic signals transmitted by nearby television stations. By turning the knobs or pressing the buttons on the front of the receiver, you select the signal from the station you wish to watch.

LOUDSPEAKER

Inside the receiver, the part of the signal carrying the picture is separated from the sound signal. The sound signal is sent to the loudspeaker. The picture signal is sent to the cathode ray tube.

SATELLITE TELEVISION

Sometimes television signals are sent from the studio to a satellite in orbit above the Earth. The satellite boosts the signals and rebroadcasts them. Dish antennas on individual homes can pick up the signals.

VIDEO CAMERA

Light passing into a video camera or camcorder falls on a microchip containing about 400,000 light detectors called charge-coupled devices (CCDs) These convert the light into an electrical signal which represents the color and brightness. The signal is then recorded as a pattern of magnetic particles on videotape. A microphone records sound on the same tape.

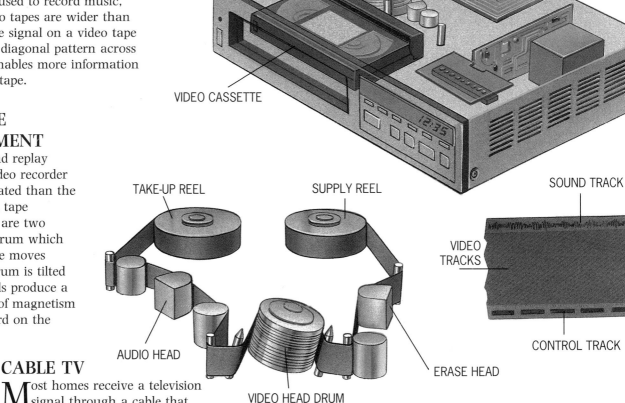

VIDEO CASSETTE

TAKE-UP REEL

SUPPLY REEL

SOUND TRACK

VIDEO TRACKS

AUDIO HEAD

ERASE HEAD

VIDEO HEAD DRUM

CONTROL TRACK

ANTENNA

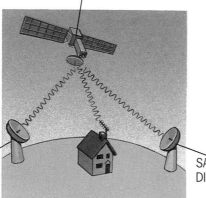

SATELLITE

TELEVISION TRANSMITTER

SATELLITE DISH

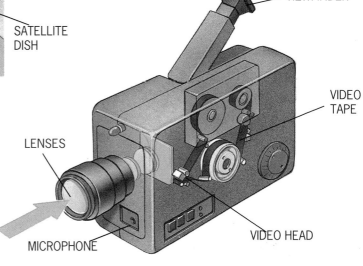

VIEWFINDER

VIDEO TAPE

LENSES

VIDEO HEAD

MICROPHONE

The sound of music

Sounds and music can be stored on discs or tape. The phonograph record stores music or speech as a spiral groove in a plastic disc, and the sounds are reproduced by a record player. The compact disc or CD stores sounds as a pattern of tiny holes on a silver metal disc. The tape recorder stores sounds as a magnetic pattern on plastic tape.

CASSETTE CASING

MAGNETIC TAPE

TAPE RECORDER

To produce a tape recording, the sound is first converted into an electrical signal by a microphone. The electrical signal is taken to the recording head in the recorder. The tape, which is covered with a thin coating of magnetic material, is passed along very close to the recording head. The magnetic material on the tape is magnetized. To play back the recording, the tape is moved past a similar head called the replay head. As the tape goes past the head, the magnetized parts of the tape cause a signal in the coil of the head. The signal is then amplified and passed to the loudspeaker.

BATTERIES

PLAYBACK HEAD

SPINDLES FOR TURNING TAPE

PERSONAL STEREO

The personal stereo or Walkman is a small portable tape player. It works in the same way as an ordinary cassette player. Some personal stereos can record music, too. The Walkman was launched in Japan in June 1979. Since then, more than 100 million of these small machines have been sold worldwide.

SOUND OUTPUT LEAD

THE RECORD PLAYER

In a record player, the record rests on a revolving table, called a turntable. A stylus or needle rests in the groove of the record. The stylus is held in a device called a cartridge, at the end of the pickup arm. The signal produced by the cartridge is fed to an electronic circuit, called an amplifier. The amplifier strengthens the signal before sending it to the loudspeaker.

RECORD

TURNTABLE

PICKUP ARM PIVOT

SPEED CONTROL BUTTONS

MOTOR

CARTRIDGE (HOLDING STYLUS)

The stylus or needle is made of sapphire or diamond. As the record turns, the needle vibrates against the bumps in the groove. The tiny vibrations of the needle cause the pickup cartridge to produce an electric current or signal which varies in step with the recorded music or words.

STYLUS

GROOVE

PITS IN DISC SURFACE

LASER BEAM

A compact disc or CD is about 4³/₄ inches across but it holds an hour of uninterrupted music. The music on the disc is stored as a spiral of tiny holes, instead of a groove. The music track can be over 12 miles long, and the turns of the spiral are so close together that 60 tracks would fit into the width of a single groove of an ordinary LP record.

PICK UP CASING

MAGNET

COIL

STYLUS

A common kind of pickup contains a small magnet held near a wire coil. As the stylus bumps along the groove, its movements shake the magnet, producing an electric signal in the coil.

COMPACT DISC

COMPACT DISC

Compact discs produce 'digital' sound - so-called because it is stored as a series of numbers, or digits, on the disc. The numbers are coded using only two signals, represented by 'reflection' or 'no reflection', produced when the laser beam shines on the disc.

LENS

PRISM

LENS

LIGHT SENSITIVE DETECTOR

LASER

The music stored on a CD is read by a laser beam shining from underneath. The laser beam is reflected off the disc if it does not shine on a hole in the disc. A system of lenses and mirrors directs the reflected beam to a light-sensitive device. After amplification, the signals are changed into the original sounds.

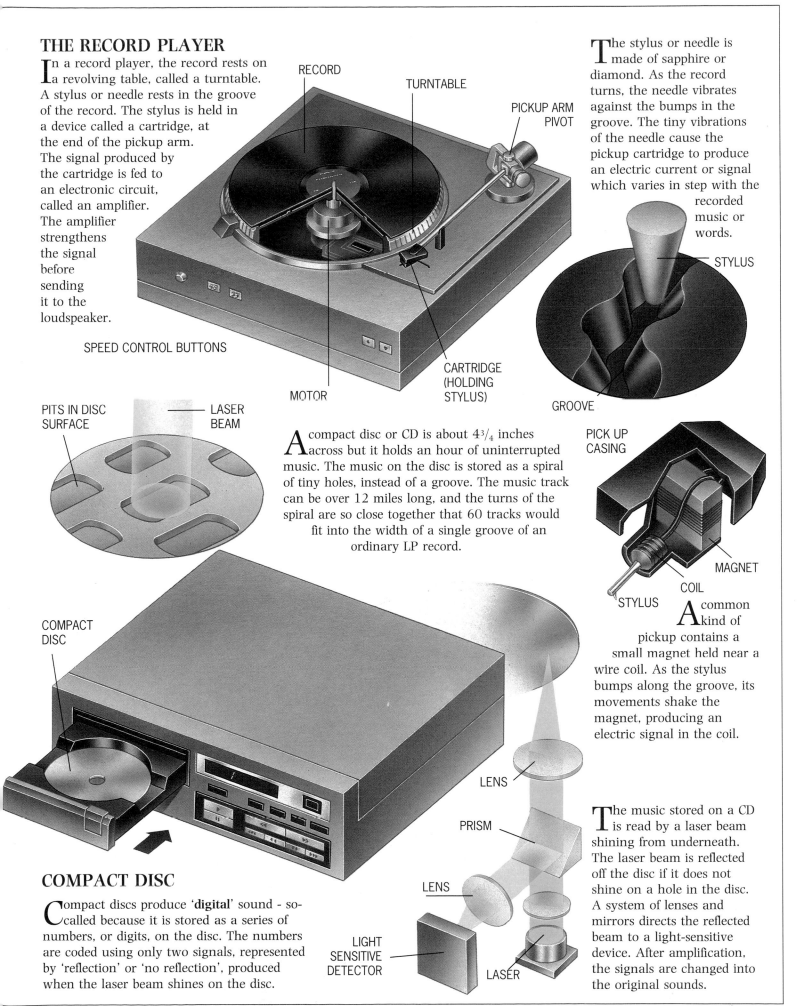

The telephone

The first telephone call was made on 10 March 1876. Inventor, Alexander Graham Bell, spoke to his assistant who was in another room. He said, "Mr Watson, please come here; I want you." There are now 700 million telephones in the world, scattered over the entire globe. About 600 billion telephone calls are made world wide each year.

HOW A TELEPHONE WORKS

The electrical signal produced by the mouthpiece is mixed with another signal, called a carrier wave, before it is sent along the telephone line. This is done because the carrier wave is a rapidly-changing signal that travels more easily along the telephone cable. At the receiving end of the telephone line, the electrical signal that is carrying the message is separated from the carrier wave. It is then amplified, or made stronger, and sent to the earpiece.

LOCAL CALLS

From the home or office, telephone signals travel to the local exchange over a pair of wires called the local loop. If the call is a local one, the local exchange will direct it to its destination.

THE MOUTHPIECE

The mouthpiece contains a microphone. When you speak into the mouthpiece, your voice makes the microphone vibrate, producing an electric signal which varies in time with the sound waves.

THE EARPIECE

The earpiece contains a small loudspeaker that converts the electrical signals into sound. The signals pass through a coil of wire which vibrates and you hear the vibrations as sound.

EARPIECE (LOUDSPEAKER)

MOUTHPIECE (MICROPHONE)

PUSH BUTTON

CIRCUIT BOARD

WALL PLUG

LONG DISTANCE CALLS

If the call is not a local one, it will be automatically directed to the local exchange nearest its destination. Each digit in a telephone number is really a code indicating where the call should be directed. For instance, if the number begins with 0, the call is automatically directed to the long distance exchange which is connected to distant parts of the country. The next few digits of the number will be used to direct the call to the next exchange.

FAX MACHINE

A facsimile machine, or fax, sends pictures or written messages along telephone lines. The earliest fax machines took six minutes to transmit a single sheet of paper. Modern machines take less than 30 seconds. This means it is quicker, and cheaper, to fax a long message than dictate it over the phone.

PRINTED DOCUMENT

PAPER ROLL

RECEIVING A FAX

The receiving fax machine contains a printer which copies the original picture line by line, printing a dot wherever the original picture is light.

THERMAL PRINT HEAD

FLUORESCENT LAMP

LENS

MIRROR

MOBILE PHONES

All the mobile phones in a local area, called a 'cell', are linked to a radio transmitter in the area. When a call is made, the caller is connected to the transmitter. The call is then sent over telephone lines to another transmitter near the person being called, and then transmitted by radio to the recipient. Each transmitter uses a different radio frequency.

DOCUMENT

PAPER ROLLER

SENDING A FAX

A fax machine scans the picture or written page, line by line, measuring the brightness of each point on the page. The machine then sends a stream of information along the telephone line, representing the brightness at each point on the page.

ANSWERING MACHINE

A telephone answering machine is a combined telephone and cassette tape recorder. The cassette contains two thin magnetic tapes. One tape holds the message which the caller hears if the telephone is not answered. This tape returns to its original position, and the message repeats each time someone calls. The second tape records the messages left by the callers.

TELEPHONE LINK

RADIO LINK

CELL TRANSMITTER/ RECEIVER

MOBILE PHONE

TAPE CASSETTE

CONTROL PANEL

OGM REC
OGM PLAY

REW
FF

PLAY/PAUSE

Clocks & watches

Clocks and watches need to be well made. No other household gadget is expected to work every second of the day, every day of the year, for years on end. Mechanical clocks and watches are so well made that they only lose a few seconds each day. Quartz clocks are even more accurate; they lose only a fraction of a second each day. But the most accurate clock of all is an atomic clock - controlled by vibrating atoms - at the US Naval Research laboratory, Washington, DC. It is estimated to lose only one second in 1,700,000 years.

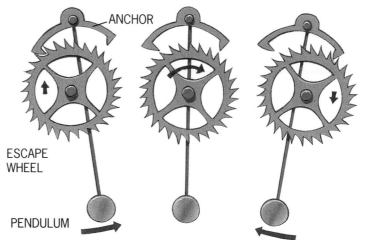

MECHANICAL TIMEKEEPING

Mechanical clocks and watches look complicated, full of cogwheels and springs. But they really have only two main parts. The first part which turns the hands is called the drive wheel. The drive wheel is turned by an unwinding spring. The second part makes sure that the drive wheel turns at a steady pace, so that the clock keeps good time. This part is called the **escapement**. The cogwheels in a clock merely connect the drive wheel to the hands, and the escapement to the drive wheel.

The escapement consists of a wheel, called the balance wheel, which moves back and forth at a regular rate, powered by a thin spring called the hair spring. The balance wheel is connected to a lever with teeth that fit into a cogged wheel, called the escape wheel. Each time the lever moves, it releases the escape wheel for a short time. This allows the main spring to move the hands.

TICK TOCK

Each time the lever rocks back and forth, it allows the escape wheel to turn by half a tooth space. Then the lever clicks back against the wheel, stopping its rotation. The 'tick tock' sound of a watch is made by the lever as it clicks against the escape wheel.

TURNING HANDS

The hands of a clock are turned by the energy of an unwinding spring, called the mainspring. The mainspring is connected to a series of toothed wheels, or gearwheels, which connect to the hands. As the spring unwinds, the gears turn the hands. The number of teeth on each gearwheel is such that the minute hand moves 12 times around the dial for each turn of the hour hand.

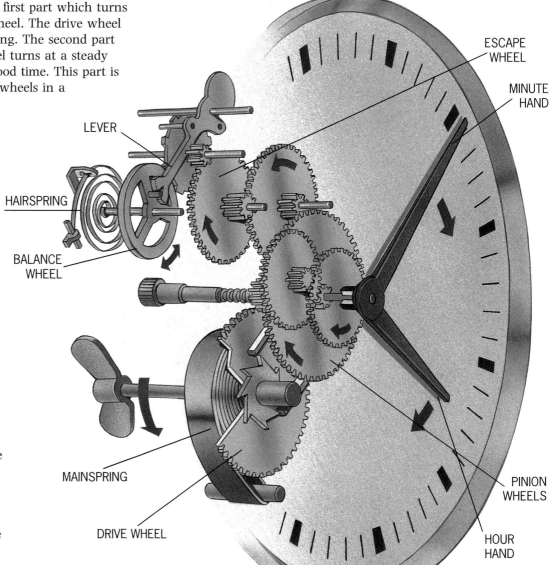

ANCHOR ESCAPEMENT

In a **pendulum** clock, the swinging pendulum rocks an 'anchor' back and forth. The anchor stops the escape wheel moving, except for a short time during each swing. Each time the anchor rocks back and forth, it gives the pendulum a tiny push in order to keep it swinging.

ends of ANCHOR TEETH engage ESCAPE WHEEL

ANCHOR

DIGITAL LIQUID CRYSTAL DISPLAY

QUARTZ CRYSTAL MICROCHIP

ESCAPE WHEEL

DIGITAL WATCH

In a digital watch, a small crystal of quartz is made to vibrate by an electric current. The crystal vibrates at a very precise rate, many thousands of times each second. The vibrations produce a very accurate electrical signal. This is used by a silicon microchip to work the digital display.

DRIVE WHEEL

BATTERIY

WEIGHT PULLS DRIVE WHEEL

GRANDFATHER CLOCK

A grandfather clock uses a pendulum to keep good time. The pendulum is a weight at the end of a metal rod. The pendulum swings back and forth, taking the same time for each swing and regulating the clock. When the drive wheel is free to move, a weight connected to it falls. This turns the drive wheel and hands.

PENDULUM

WATCH FACTS

◆ The earliest time keeping systems divided daylight and night time into periods of 12 hours each. This meant that the length of each hour changed during the year as nights lengthened and shortened.

◆ The Babylonians, in about 3000 B.C. were the first to make all 24 hours of equal length. In Europe equal hours were not used until 1350, many years after the introduction of the first mechanical clocks.

◆ Summer 1992 was longer than usual – by one second. An extra second was added to the world's time at precisely 23 hours, 59 minutes and 60 seconds on June 30 in order to keep super–accurate atomic clocks in step with the Earth's rotation.

Glossary

ALTERNATING CURRENT An electric current that flows first in one direction and then in the opposite direction.

AMPÈRE The unit used to measure the size of an electric current. It is named after the French scientist André Ampère (1775-1836).

BIMETALLIC STRIP Two flat strips of different metals joined together so that the strip bends when the temperature changes.

CARRIER WAVE A radio wave with which a signal is mixed before being broadcast.

CATHODE RAY TUBE A glass tube in which a stream of electrons is shot at a fluorescent screen, making it glow.

COMPUTER MEMORY The part of a computer that stores the set of instructions, or program, and the information the computer needs during its work.

CONDUCTION The process that allows electricity or heat to flow through a substance. All metals are conductors.

CONVECTION The way heat travels through a gas or liquid as currents of heated material. The hot gas or liquid rises to the top, the cold sinks to the bottom.

CONVEX LENS OR MIRROR A lens or mirror that is curved outwards. The outside of a shiny spoon forms a convex mirror.

COOLANT A substance, such as ammonia, circulated in a refrigerator to produce a low temperature as it evaporates.

CRANK A device, consisting of a rod fixed to a wheel, which converts a turning movement into a back and forth movement.

DEMODULATION The process, used in radio broadcasting, of separating the carrier wave and the signal.

DIGITAL SIGNAL A signal that is represented in the form of numbers (digits). Digital sound, for example, is music or speech recorded as a sequence of numbers.

DIRECT CURRENT An electric current that flows in one direction, and does not reverse its flow as alternating current does. The electricity produced by a battery is direct current.

ELECTRIC CIRCUIT A pathway along which electricity can flow. Electricity cannot flow unless it has a complete pathway or circuit.

ELECTRIC CURRENT A flow of electrons through a wire or other conductor.

ELECTROMAGNET An iron bar with coils of wire around it. It acts as a magnet when an electric current flows through the wire.

ELECTROMAGNETIC RADIATION Energy that travels through empty space at the speed of light. There is a wide range of electromagnetic radiations, including light, X-rays and radio waves.

ELECTRON A tiny electrically-charged particle. An electric current is a flow of electrons.

ESCAPEMENT The part of a clock mechanism which ensures that the clock keeps good time.

FLOPPY DISC A small plastic disc with a magnetic coating used to store information for a computer.

FOCAL POINT The point at which light rays meet to form a sharp image after passing through a lens, or being reflected from a curved mirror.

FREQUENCY The number of repititions of an action in a given time.

GEARS OR GEARWHEELS A toothed wheel that transmits the turning movement of one shaft to a second shaft.

HARDWARE The physical parts of a computer system, such as the printer, the display screen, and the computer itself. 'Software' is the computer programs.

ION An atom, or group of atoms, which carries an electric charge.

INFRARED RAY A type of electromagnetic radiation with wavelength just longer than that of red light. It can be felt as heat.

INSULATOR A material that does not conduct heat or electricity. Many non-metals, such as rubber and plastics, are insulators.

INTEGRATED CIRCUIT A complete electronic circuit built on a small piece, called a chip, of semiconductor material such as silicon.

LASER A device that produces a powerful narrow beam of light. Lasers are used in medicine, industry and in CD players.

LENS A piece of glass or transparent material that has curved surfaces. Light passing through a lens is bent and can form an image. Lenses are used in cameras, microscopes and telescopes.

LIQUID CRYSTAL DISPLAY The type of display used in digital watches. They use liquid crystals, materials that are halfway between liquids and solids, because these become visible when an electric current passes through them.

MAGNETRON An electronic device that generates microwaves. They are used in microwave ovens, for example.

MICROPROCESSOR An integrated circuit that contains most of the parts of a computer on a small piece of silicon.

MICROWAVE A form of electromagnetic radiation of very short wavelength. Microwaves are used in communications (e.g. radio) and in cooking.

MODULATION The process, used in radio broadcasting, of adding a signal to a carrier wave before broadcasting.

MOUSE A computer input device which, when moved over the desktop, moves a pointer on the computer screen.

OBJECTIVE LENS The front, largest lens in a telescope or microscope.

PENDULUM A weight (called a bob) swinging at the end of a rod, or cord. The regularity of a pendulum's swing was used in making the first accurate clocks in the 17th century.

PERMANENT MAGNET A magnet which retains its magnetism under normal circumstances.

PHOSPHOR A material which glows when it receives energy; for example, after being hit with electrons.

RADIATION Energy which can travel through empty space as electromagnetic waves, such as light, radio, X-rays, or as particles, such as neutrons.

SERVICE ENTRANCE CABLE The cable which carries electricity into a home, office or factory from the main supply.

SILICON CHIP Another name for an integrated circuit; a complete electronic circuit built on a small piece, called a chip, of silicon.

SOFTWARE The program (list of instructions) and data (information) which are fed into a computer.

THERMOSTAT A device which can regulate the temperature of an oven or refrigerator.

VACUUM An empty space, that contains no air or other material.

VOLTAGE The electrical pressure in a circuit, which drives the electrical current around the circuit. The pressure is measured in volts, named after an Italian scientist Alessandro Volta (1745-1827).

WAVELENGTH The distance between two successive peaks or troughs of a wave.

Index